What if Today Were the Day?

Book four of the Giggle Yoga Series

First Pocket Book

David Lloyd Strauss

July 2021

Dedicated to my mom,

Marianne Jacqueline Strauss,

who died at the
young age of
thirty-nine.

I love you mom.

Time heals the tears,
but the pain
never goes away.

What if today were your lucky day?

V

you realized you have
all the love, strength,
and courage you need
to overcome any obstacle,
pursue any dream, and be
the person you are
fully capable of being?

What if today were the day
you gathered up the
courage and declared
this moment to be
a turning point
in your life?

What if today were the day
you finally looked in the
mirror and realized
how beautiful
and powerful
you are?

What if today were the day
you let go of all your
excuses, petty distractions,
and senseless blame,
and began to
love and accept
yourself just
as you are?

What if today were the day
you stopped suffering
in silence and instead,
raised your standards
of what is and is not
acceptable
to you.

What if today were the day
you said no to what you
do not want and yes
to what you do want?

What if today were the day
you started believing
in yourself and no longer
needed the validation
of others?

What if today were the day you realized that being happy, healthy, and prosperous is a choice?

What if today were the day
you allowed true love into
your life—for yourself
and another?

What if today were the day you acknowledged that none of us are perfect— that we all have strengths and weaknesses, and you stopped judging and started accepting?

What if today were the day
you stopped focusing on
everyone's differences
and appreciated what
we have in common?

What if today were the day you remembered that we are all a part of the same family of humanity?

What if today were the day
you recognized we are
all one. We are not apart
from each other but
a part of each other?

What if today were the day
you realized that whatever
you do to yourself, you do
to others, and whatever
you do to others,
you also do to yourself?

What if today were the day
you rescued yourself first so
that you could be free
to bless and serve others?

What if today were the day
you realized your life will not
go on forever, and you
chose to live each day
with appreciation,
humility, and heart?

What if today were the day
you accepted complete
responsibility for your life
and pursued your dreams
without fear of
judgment or failure?

What if this moment, right now, is the intersection in time where your dreams started to become your reality, and you began to notice what you do have rather than focusing on what you do not have?

What if today were the day you stopped buying your excuses and started believing in yourself?

What if today were the day you stopped living in the past and worrying about the future, and you began to appreciate the power of here and now?

What if today were the day
you contributed to others
without the expectation of
receiving anything
in return?

What if today were the day you prayed words of gratitude rather than words of need?

If today were the day,
what would your new life
look and feel like?

How would you
treat others?

What difference would
you make in the world?

Who would you forgive?

What would you let go of?

What would you create?

Today can be the day.

Today can be the day you declare, once and for all, that you own your life, and you are going to do everything you can to release past hurts and pains, get focused on your dreams, and begin to create the reality you choose.

Despite all obstacles, challenges, and distractions, you are allowed to create your oasis of happiness.

You are allowed to feel completely blessed and overjoyed with your life, and grateful for every miracle you experience.

You do not need anyone's
permission to be yourself,
to be happy
and to feel loved.

You only need
your permission.

You do not need to fit in
and be accepted by others
in order to be happy.

You need to accept
yourself and stand out by
being authentic and
making a difference.

There is only a limited
amount of time to live
the remainder
of your life.

Do not assume
you will have a tomorrow.

You have no idea when
you will breathe your
final breath, smell your
last flower, cry your last
teardrop, or giggle your
final morsel of happiness.

You will always have more dreams than you will have time for them to come true.

Establish your priorities.

Decide what is most
important to you in life
and make it your
purpose and passion.

Develop healthy
relationships that support
and challenge you
to learn and grow.

Discover the magic
of the moment
and the beauty
of a smile.

Forgive quickly.

Dance often.

Be
unapologetically
yourself.

Be hungry
for everything
life has to offer.

Be flexible with your
thoughts and beliefs.

Open your heart
to possibilities.

Be the blessing
you are looking for.

Be the hero of your life.

Accept complete
responsibility for your
happiness, health,
and prosperity.

Inspire others
to do the same.

Let today be the day
you begin to believe in your
potential—begin to live the
life you love with giggles,
gratitude, and a fierce
smile packed
with enthusiasm.

Do all this and more,
and you will become
the master of your life.

***

This, my friend,
is the path of
Giggle Yoga.

***

Pray. Give Thanks.

Giggle Out Loud.

Giggle Often.

GiggleYoga.com

About the Author

David Strauss became inspired to write after recovering from a rockfall to his head while visiting ancient Anasazi ruins in Chaco Canyon, New Mexico.

The turbulence of life is familiar to David. As a result of the in-fighting in his family after the death of his mother at a young age, David ran away from home when he was fifteen so that he could find peace, discover who he is, and build a life for himself.

To make sense of his life, David became an avid reader and world traveler. He discovered that life is a mirror. There is no truth outside of your own heart and mind.

You can travel all the continents, dive the deepest of oceans and ascend the highest peaks, and you will never find the truth.

The last place you look is where you will discover all that you are looking for—in your heart.

It is within your heart you will find gratitude, joy, healing, forgiveness, peace of mind, grace, abundance, and most importantly, your unique relationship with the divine.

Through the openness of his heart, David has become a globally known author, thought leader, and life strategist.

David has been seen on ABC, NBC, CBS, and FOX affiliate networks and presented at a private event at the

United Nations Headquarters in New York City.

David believes that you are never truly free until you release all blame and accept complete responsibility for your entire life.

***

Watch David's videos on social media.

David's coaching programs can be found on his website.

Invite David to speak at your event.

davidstrauss.com

@davidlloydstrauss

#davidlloydstrauss

David's other Books

Order all of David's books online through most online booksellers including:

Amazon.com

BarnesAndNobel.com

- Dancing with Vampires
- Footsteps After the Fall
- Second Mouse Gets the Cheese

CPSIA information can be obtained
at www.ICGtesting.com
Printed in the USA
LVHW052357080522
717900LV00004B/75